CANADA'S
NORTHWEST TERRITORIES
A Land of Diversity

BY

LESLIE LEONG

Dedicated to my sons Tynan and Makinen,
with the hope that wild spaces like these
will survive for their generation to be a part
of in the future.

Leslie Leong ENT. LTD.

National Library of Canada Cataloguing in Publication
Leong, Leslie, 1962-
    Canada's Northwest Territories : a land of diversity / by Leslie Leong.
Part of text previously published under title: Our forgotten north.
ISBN 0-9681715-5-9

    1. Northwest Territories--Pictorial works. I. Leong, Leslie, 1962- .
Our forgotten north. II. Title.

FC4161.L45 2003   971.9'3'00222   C2003-901768-0
F1060.L45 2003

Published in Canada by Leslie Leong Ent. Ltd.
Box 1372, Fort Smith, Northwest Territories XOE OPO

Acknowledgments
My thanks to all the people who helped make this book a reality. Their support and assistance was essential. Particular thanks are due to Nigel Allan, our sons and Amy Griffiths for taking care of our life when I most needed it; to Detmar Schwichtenberg, a faithful editor who taught me much about writing over the years; to Ib Christensen & Judith Drinnan, NWT booksellers that never stop encouraging me; Nancy Wise at Sandhill Book Marketing Ltd. for good advice and distribution; to Andy Kauffman at Kromar Printing for giving the book everything he could; to Alex Hall of Canoe Arctic, Christian Boucher, Jane Chisholm, Robyn Allan, Kris Schlagintweit, Petr Cizek, Timothy Warren Ruben, Helene at DOT, Liz Danielson, Janet Lanoville at Aurora College Library, Doug Camsel at NTCL, NWT fire Centre, and the City of Yellowknife for technical advice; to Steve Catto, Peggy Jay, and Kim Hastie, among others, for photos. I also thank my travelling companions through the years. Without them, I would not have the images to fill these pages.

A special thanks is due to Jim Excel, Denise Burlingame and BHP-Billiton. Their critical support made the book a larger representation of the Northwest Territories. I remain grateful to all those who helped with the first book, *Our Forgotten North*, and all those who supported this new book by buying that book. Lastly I apologize to my friends and family for neglecting our relationships while preparing this book.

Cover Photo: *Terry Wolfe and his team of dogs return from an afternoon run.*
Title Page: *Rock cranberry are one of the most relished edible northern plants. Their berries ripen after the first frosts and are reputedly most delectable in the spring, after having past the long winter under the snow.*
Above: *The aurora borealis fill the sky over Kozo Lake. A strip of land marks the horizon.*

On initial sighting, lynx tend to vanish into the folds of the boreal forest. On this occasion, there was a family of five, two of which were more curious than the others. In some locations, a lynx is refered to as 'link', likely derived from the early oral understanding of the English language, 'links' being more than one link.

The central barrenlands are the calving grounds for the Beverly caribou herd. In fall they migrate into the treeline for winter.

Photo: Alex Hall of Canoe Arctic

This map is based on information taken from MCR 101, the Atlas of Canada.
© 2003. Her Majesty the Queen in Right of Canada with permission of Natural Resources Canada.

NORTHWEST
TERRITORIES

CANADA

All-season Roads
Winter Roads
Northwest Territories
Boundary
Water
Sea Level to 300 metres
300 to 700 metres
700 to 1500 metres
over 1500 metres
NATIONAL PARKS
Bird and Wildlife Sanctuaries
Approximate Limit of Trees

NORTHWEST

NUNAVUT

TERRITORIES

YUKON

YELLOWKNIFE

Introduction

The Cessna spins dizzily to improve our perspective of the islands of spruce, like a bird of prey seeking a better view of a scuttling mouse, and I think as we spin that the patches of green capture the essence of the Salt Plains in a single image. The surrounding mud flats, too bare and saline for plant life to grow, lap like a vast and desolate ocean at the shores of the salt-stressed islands. Like Yin and Yang, you cannot have a sense of one without the other.

It is autumn in Wood Buffalo National Park and evening sunlight warms the sparse autumn foliage and wisps of reddened mud, while exaggerated shadows emphasize the silhouettes of spruce trees, symbol of the boreal forest.

I remember the overcast day when I heard thumping footsteps outside the tent and, expecting to see my prankster companion, I peered out the crack in the screen window. Instead I found a long snout covered in short, fine golden hairs and tipped by a black nose close enough to touch. Our eyes did not meet. I jumped back and paused to collect my racing thoughts. Then I grabbed the 'bear scare' and my camera and leapt out of the tent but the bear had already run beyond the next beach.

A tin shack marks Coal Mine on the Hornaday River. In the recent past, people came by dog team to harvest coal from the exposed coal seams to heat their homes. The extraordinary lapidary collection is enhanced by unusually heavy, molten boulders that smell of metal filings.

Downstream we discover freezer-sized boulders that look like clusters of huge bubbles rising from a giant's bath. Some rocks have a metallic luster in rich colours, like Raku pottery, while other gigantic concretions resemble fat flying saucers that dwarf a human being. I have never seen such a variety of unusual rocks and formations.

The diversity of my experiences in the wild landscape of the Northwest Territories (NWT) says much about the territory itself: the people and culture, the plants and animals, the geology and geography. The photographic journey through this incredible diversity is presented in three sections.

The first section focuses on the human imprint on the land, the second on the arctic mainland and the high arctic islands, and the third on the two-thirds of the NWT below the treeline. Traditional activities tied to the natural environment are included in all three sections.

Most of this magnificent land is still wild and untouched but development, for better and worse, continues to expand into untouched wilderness. Humans are part of the environment and development services the needs and desires of the people but everything is forever bigger, faster and 'better'. Some, like the Deh Cho First Nation, ask how much development is appropriate. How fast, they want to know, and why now? Natural resources are not perishable, they say, and perhaps it is better to wait until the people need them.

The Human Imprint on the Land

After a 425-kilometre flight we set up camp ten days' hike from a community of 300 people on the shore of the Arctic Ocean. It seems remote yet just up the slope is a bluff that contains fourteen meat caches among crevasses, boulders and slabs of rock used in times before oral history. I crawl inside one crevasse to find a damp, mossy darkness and I am awed at the ingenuity of these early people. Back at camp my travel companions introduce me to the sweet, tart leaves of mountain sorrel, similar in taste to apple peel. I realize then that my companions are likely ancestors of those who built the meat caches.

About half the people in the NWT are aboriginal and the entire society is strongly influenced by aboriginal culture. Non-aboriginal people are mostly southerners who come to seek adventure or work.

Many initially resist the ways of the North and then come to either love the place or hate it, without much in between.

Some are odd, reclusive types who find 1.17 million square kilometers of diverse landscape a perfect place to hide from a world they do not like or understand. They find refuge in the wilderness or the isolated settlements and hamlets that dot even the most remote regions, or find their way to the three larger towns of a few thousand people. Almost half the 40,000 people who inhabit the NWT live in the capital of Yellowknife. It is a small drop in a country of over 31 million people.

Houseboats scattered in Yellowknife Bay are self sufficient, running on solar and wind power, heated by wood stoves and propane space heaters. Sewage and household waste is disposed of manually at designated sites provided by the City of Yellowknife. The channel in the Bay is also used by float planes as a runway. Houseboat residents can feel the wake of the planes created by take-off and landing.

Upper Left: *Dancers with drums create silhouettes in a fire lit teepee.*
Upper Right: *Natasha and Marion Green are bright-eyed in the night sun.*
Lower: *Mary Cazon prepares wild duck for a campfire meal out on the land.*

The setting sun illustrates the peacefulness of the landscape which is imbibed by the people while out on the land.

Smoke filled skies in Yellowknife Bay are caused by winds carrying smoke from forest fires across the Canadian Shield. The summer's fire season is sure to keep seasonal workers busy out on the land.

Upper: *Boats provide summer access for houseboat residents. In winter, they can drive up to their doorstep over lake ice.*
Lower: *Black bears are usually, but not always, black.*

Yellowknife has its origins in a few log cabins on Joliffe and Latham Islands, and one of the first streets in the old town was Ragged Ass Road but the sign keeps getting stolen faster than it can be replaced. Now the polished sheen of architectural steel and glass at the Legislative Assembly stands in stark contrast to squatter shacks made from recycled materials scavenged mainly from the city dump.

The city motto is *multum in parvo*, which means "much in a small place," and today Yellowknife behaves like a big city, despite a population of only 17,000. Eclectic sub-cultures include everything from society drop-outs to crusty old prospectors and environment-conscious professionals to conservative business people. House boats in bright colours dot the bay against a background of Canadian Shield granite outcrops that thwart the lineal development of city planners. The Shield extends east of Yellowknife, beyond the treeline 200 kilometres away and into the tundra.

A sundog sky silhouettes the Pilot's Monument, overlooking Yellowknife Bay in winter's grip.

Upper Left: *The construction of an ice castle has become an annual event.*
Upper Right: *Snowmobiles give residents access to the land in winter.*
Lower: *The Legislative Assembly of the Northwest Territories in Yellowknife.*

Photo: Jiri Hermann/courtesy of BHP-Billiton

Upper: *Ekati was the first diamond mine in the Northwest Territories.*
Lower: *The Wildcat Cafe, built in 1937, still operates each summer in the original heritage building.*

Upper Left: *Protection from bugs is essential to the enjoyment of summer.*
Upper Right: *A derelict canoe lies in the grass between rock outcrops in Edzo.*
Lower: *Aurora dance over a ski plane in Yellowknife's Old Town.*

Upper: *Sand beaches are created by eskers on the shores of a Thelon Tributary.*
Lower: *On the labrador tea dotted tundra, a lack of distinct features creates the need for navigation tools.*

Lower: *A telling quote from John Hornby's diary is posted in memorium at Warden's Grove on the Thelon River. None of three ill-prepared men survived the intentional over-wintering on the Thelon River in 1927.*

Upper: *Canoeing is a common holiday adventure for northerners.*
Lower: *A Royal Canadian Mounted Police presence can be found in all northern communities.*

Upper Left: *Santa really does live in the north, and he is an avid gardener.*
Upper Right: *The fly-speckled orchid is minute but magnificent.*
Lower: *Beaded slippers are proudly worn throughout the subarctic.*

Two men curse and swear as they wrestle oversized teepee poles and reams of canvas under an electric blue sky and a vibrant orange horizon. It is well past midnight and the teepee is almost finished but something is not quite right. One man lifts the weight of the teepee off the end of a pole while the other buzzes off the excess with a chainsaw. Not a recommended safety practice.

Small tent frames are standard portable shelter in the subarctic but the teepee has special cultural significance and its symbolism brings the community together. Considerable pride goes into the erection of a teepee and I understand the drive of these two men as I wade into the water to frame the teepee and its reflection. The teepee is a striking symbol that represents their identity as First Nations people.

A collective of aboriginal groups in the subarctic is called the Dene – meaning "the people" – and represents about 25% of the total population. The subarctic is also home to many Metis, who originated from the mix of French traders and native trappers and make up less than 10% of the people in the NWT. Traditional ways are still a part of the lives of these people. Time out on the land is spiritually important and provides a significant portion of their sustenance.

Upper: *Boats are essential for access to fish stocks on the Mackenzie River.*
Middle: *The Metis Reelers take pride in their jigging performances.*
Lower: *Campfires provide a casual meeting place amongst the teepee camp.*

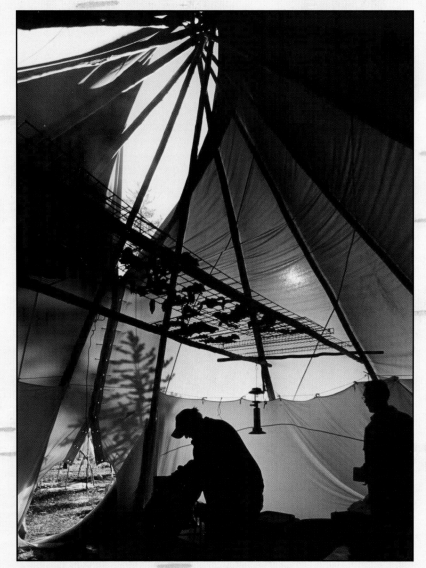

Smoke from the fire adds flavour and keeps flies away as caribou meat dries on the rack suspended inside the teepee. The meat is prepared by carefully slicing and rolling a slab out into a thin sheet.

Upper: *A cedar strip canoe rests on a beach at the base of an esker.*
Lower Left: *Mountain Avens are the official flower of the Northwest Territories.*
Lower Right: *Elder Maryrose Waquan harvests cranberries in autumn.*

Upper Left: *Grabbing a goose is not recommended, but possible during molt.*
Upper Right: *Elder Gabe Cazon sharpens his axe at his tent camp.*
Lower: *A moon rises in the sunset sky over the Redknife River.*

In the early morning light, a fire lit teepee is reflected in the lake. The teepee is a striking cultural symbol that brings the aboriginal community together.

Upper: *Cars are taken across the river by heli-lift when the ice bridge is too weak for crossing and the ice is still too thick for the ferry.*
Lower: *Roads in the Northwest Territories use ferries to cross major rivers.*

Upper Left: *Churches like this one in Fort Providence are typical in the north.*
Upper Right: *The door handle on a Lynn tractor compliments its aging paint.*
Lower: *An old Lynn tractor illustrates the rivalry between companies.*

I feel dwarfed by the ships in dry dock at the yard in Hay River's Old Town, all hauled from the water by the world's furthest inland synchrolift. The deck on one barge is so flat and expansive that it begs a ball and a game of soccer. Much of the NWT is just as flat, intersected by bodies and arteries of water that once a year provide passage for barges to bring supplies and staples to remote Arctic communities. The mammoth size of spools of cable mirror the extent and importance of this essential shipping industry to the NWT.

Transportation by water, then by road, pushed the development of the NWT. An overprint of the Hudson's Bay Co. and Ryan Brothers on an old Lynn tractor illustrates the fierce competition among rival companies. These remnants are scattered throughout the NWT and tell the story of the early days of development.

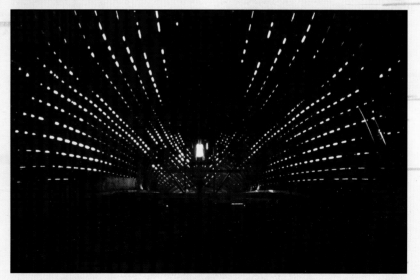

Huge spools store marine cables inside the shop in the shipyard of Hay River's Old Town.

Upper Left: *Even details of the ships in dry dock are large scale.*
Upper Right: *An abandoned boat in Old Town catches evening light.*
Lower: *Light highlights graceful curves inside the hull of the derelict boat.*

Ice fishing is a viable industry in the Simpson Islands of Great Slave Lake. Nets are set using a jigger to slide a line along the bottom of the ice.

Upper: *Wind chill in winter increases the severity of low temperatures.*
Lower: *Last year's lily pads show up again in the spring thaw.*

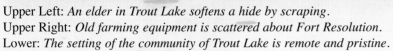

Upper Left: *An elder in Trout Lake softens a hide by scraping.*
Upper Right: *Old farming equipment is scattered about Fort Resolution.*
Lower: *The setting of the community of Trout Lake is remote and pristine.*

Upper: *The settlement of Rat River on the Taltson River is abandoned.*
Lower: *Finely crafted birch bark baskets are made by local women in Fort Liard. The baskets are often decorated with dyed porcupine quills.*

Roads bring economic benefits to northern communities but easy access to manufactured goods, processed foods and alcohol disrupt traditional ways of life. In addition the benefits are cyclical because most smaller communities are only accessible by ice road in winter.

Highways crews build ice roads by pushing snow off cleared forest routes, muskeg and marsh, and flooding areas of natural ice to form ice bridges over rivers and lakes. For several weeks in spring the ice softens but is still too thick for boats and barges so all supplies must be airlifted in at a substantial premium. This can also happen in fall when ice is not yet thick enough to support vehicles. In summer ferries cross major rivers but many communities remain accessible only by air or water.

The Dempster Highway, built to coincide with a boom in oil and gas industries, provides transport links to places like Inuvik, Tsiigehtchic and Fort McPherson.

Upper: *Fort Simpson lies on an island beside the confluence of the Liard and Mackenzie Rivers.*
Lower: *Silhouettes in the night sun clearly illustrate the structure of a teepee.*

Right: *Elder Fred Sabourin tells stories at his cabin on the Mackenzie River.*
Left: *Writer and story teller, Jim Green frosts up after a cold winter walk.*

Photo: Detmar Schwichtenberg

Photo: Kim Hastie

Upper Left: *An old saw collection decorates a shack in Norman Wells.*
Upper Right: *John Yukon of Norman Wells guides us on the river.*
Lower: *God's light on the paintings dating from 1878 in Our Lady of Good Hope.*

Upper: *The Lost Patrol: without a Dene guide, four Royal Canadian Mounted Police died in 1910 on their first patrol from Fort McPherson to Dawson City.*
Lower: *First communion is a grand event in the church in Fort Good Hope.*

22

   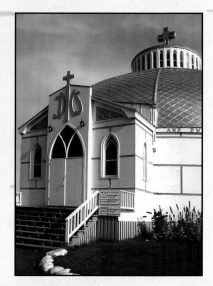

Upper Left: *The blanket toss is a traditional Inuvialuit pastime.*
Upper Right: *Judas Ullulaq was renown for raw expression in his carvings.*
Lower: *The Mackenzie River ferry connects Tsiigehtchic and the Dempster highway.*

Upper Left: *The inside of the igloo church emphasizes the dome shaped roof.*
Upper Right: *The igloo church is Inuvik's most unique building.*

Upper: *Fiddling has worked its way into northern culture.*
Lower: *A minute carving in walrus ivory is polished at Inuvik's Great Northern Arts Festival, the largest arts event in the Northwest Territories.*

Upper: *The Great Northern Arts Festival creates opportunites for everyone to try out Inuvialuit cultural activities, like the blanket toss.*
Lower: *A dancer's coat is decorated with felt applique, fur and Delta Braid.*

Upper: *The mission boat from the 1930s, Our Lady of Lourdes, permanently rests high and dry in Tuktoyuktuk.*
Lower: *Arctic cotton and pingos are part of the community of Tuktoyuktuk.*

Upper: *The Anglican church in Tuktoyuktuk is heated by wood stove in winter.*
Lower: *High priced tours follow the Northwest Passage, stopping at small communities on the shores of the Beaufort Sea.*

Upper: *Changing temperatures cause moisture to migrate within permafrost. Airborne moisture crystalizes into beautiful hexagonal ornaments of hoar frost.*
Lower: *Small rooms down in the permafrost are used as family freezers.*

Marion Green helps her father clean the fish they hauled in from the nets. Arctic char, similar to salmon, is prized for its smooth, full taste.

Arctic time runs on nature's schedule, where clocks and calendars and other human abstractions are oddly out of place.

Are the char running? Just a few spawners in the net.

Is it time? Maybe.

The elusive departure time arrives and Nelson Green and some extended family head for a camp at the mouth of the Hornaday River. There is a mock sunset but the sun never really sets and children play and help clean fish and ask for their picture to be taken. Time has a natural rhythm. The Arctic char are running and it is time to fish all night long until the quota is filled.

My natural rhythm says sleep. With my jacket as a blanket I lie on cardboard under the tent frame and sleep. I am foreign to this land, these people and their language but I am welcome, fed and cared for. That is a natural way of the North.

Upper Left: *Inuvialuit girls are accustomed to caring for younger siblings.*
Upper Right: *Nelson Green hauls in arctic char from his net near Paulatuk.*
Lower: *A tundra camp catches the evening sun.*

Laura from Tuktoyuktuk prepares fish for drying using an ulu, a traditional Inuvialuit knife. The bones are removed and the flesh is sliced into small sections to allow rapid drying. The flesh is still attached to the skin for hanging.

Photo: Peggy Jay

Photo: Steve Catto

Upper: *The community of Holman forms a crescent around Queen's Bay.*
Lower: *Ptarmigan in winter camouflage almost disappear in the snow.*

Upper Left: *Eli Nasogaluak is a renown carver from Tuktoyuktuk.*
Upper Right: *The airport fence makes a great stretcher for seal hide.*
Lower: *The historical monument overlooks the community of Sachs Harbour.*

The mouth of the Hornaday River forms expansive shallows in the ocean. Boats carefully and slowly wind their way along channels with slightly deeper water. Winds keep the open water on the ocean too rough to travel quickly and safely.

Beyond the Treeline: The Arctic Mainland and High Arctic Islands

The river unfurls like a turquoise satin ribbon. Steep rock walls rise from the river and stop abruptly where the endless tundra begins. Deep magenta Arctic fireweed and pale purple petals of Siberian aster grow at my feet, sheltered for a moment from unrelenting wind. The hike has been easy except for the unaccustomed load on my back. My reward is the clear, powerful water that winds back and forth and disappears between sheer cliffs that fold into the tundra at the loft of the canyon.

The Arctic is beautiful and extreme, big and harsh. The summer sun does not set and skies are clear blue. I cover up head to toe but I have nothing for my hands and they develop an itchy rash. There are no trees and the sun never stops. I crawl under a meager shrub of willow to find shade. In winter the wind is constant and snow blankets the land and the sea ice. Temperatures often reach - 40°C.

Two men asleep in a cabin awake to find the stove has lit the cabin on fire and they escape with nothing but the clothes they wear. They drive 100 kilometres by snowmobile. One man makes it back but the other freezes to death *en route*. He was an experienced, capable man who took me fishing last summer, but nature does not discriminate.

The land provides plentiful fish and game but also the harshest climate humans anywhere endure. The Arctic is raw, devoid of protective cover. There is nowhere to hide from the incredible power of nature.

Left: *Frank Wolki, at the top, Marion and Natsha Green, and Logan Ruben travelled by boat from Paulatuk to the family fishing camp in June.*
Right: *Bog Rosemary occurs in wet tundra on the arctic mainland.*

Driftwood from the Beaufort Sea is propped up to provide protection from the wind. In the 19th century, Inuvialuit built large multi-family houses using driftwood and mud.

Upper: *This 45 metre high pingo near Tuktoyuktuk is pure ice through its core.*
Lower: *Permafrost is ground that remains frozen all year. The permafrost under Tuktoyuktuk is mostly frozen water with just a light swirl of sand.*

The Inuvialuit – many of them ancestors of migrants from Alaska – lived in multi-family houses made of mud and driftwood, using snow houses in transit. They traveled back and forth along the Arctic coast to trap fox in Sachs Harbour, catch fish and hunt in Aklavik in the Mackenzie Delta, and trade with the Dene. Their livelihood depended on whale hunting and Herschel Island was a regular stop between the Alaskan coast and the NWT. The camp became a supply post, whaling station and North-West Mounted Police Post for over two decades.

I met Tuktoyuktuk elder Persis Grueben on Herschel Island. She recalls using sticks and rocks as dolls and playing in the snow banks between the buildings in the not-so-distant whaling days. Her home town got its name when a woman, seeing offshore reefs on the horizon, mistook them for caribou and thereafter the reefs were called Tuktoyuktuk, which means "resembling caribou."

I am told Tuktoyuktuk will sink if the Arctic becomes too warm. I only understand the magnitude of this information when I visit the community freezer. We descend 30 or more ladder rungs into the depths of the permafrost and a tunnel with doors, each of which is a freezer belonging to one family. I run my hands over the mass of dark ice and find it smooth and cold and partly granular to touch. The proportion of sand is very small, like butterscotch swirls in a bucket of ice cream.

Upper: *Whalers' graves stand erect over the tundra foliage on Herschel Island.*
Lower: *Learning and playing at the family traditional camp is commonplace in the lives of Inuvialuit children like Nicole and Natasha Green and Logan Ruben.*

Upper: *Herschel Island hosts a colony of Guillemots.*
Middle: *The RCMP buildings and warehouses date back to the early 1900s.*
Lower: *Northern Whaling & Trading Co. warehouse on Hershel Island.*

At S-Bend Canyon I am completely surrounded by sheer walls on the Hornaday River except for one slender, precipitous avenue back to the tundra. The canyon closes in and the opposite wall beckons me to reach out and touch it. I feel almost dizzy as I stand on the edge at such height.

The first waterfall has no name but is magnificent in an intimate way. The river exits the monolithic bluffs sliced into the tundra. Then layered slabs of fossilized rock in beige, pink and mint squeeze the river where the canyon does a hair-pin turn and pours raging foam into an enormous bowl worn smooth by flow over time immemorial. I sit and feel the immense energy of the water, the gentle mist on my face and the intense Arctic sun on my back. The constant but ever-changing flow of water mesmerizes me and I feel I am at the heart of the river.

At La Ronciére Falls the river drops over a wide angular ledge interrupted by alcoves and notches in the rock face. The result is spectacular yet delicate. In one box cut into the ledge just off-centre, the water flows in from three sides, while the fourth side is partially blocked, throwing the water back on itself and creating rainbows in the evening sun. The perfect end to a day in Tuktut Nogait National Park.

Upper Left: *Net-veined Willow leaves burst through a clump of moss-campion.*
Upper Right: *A canyon of bluffs, boulders and slabs on the Hornaday River.*
Lower: *A meat cache on the Hornaday River in Tuktut Nogait National Park.*

Monolithic bluffs line the edge of the Hornaday River upstream of renown La Ronciére Falls. The river cuts through Tuktut Nogait National Park near Paulatuk. With numerous canyons and waterfalls, it is the Grand Canyon of the north.

Upper: *La Ronciére Falls is the most significant feature of the Hornaday River. It lies within Tuktut Nogait National Park.*
Lower: *The intimate First Falls result from spectacular bluffs and projections.*

Upper Left: *The spray of La Ronciére Falls creates a rainbow in the arctic sun.*
Upper Right: *Sicsics, or arctic ground squirrels, are common on the tundra.*
Lower: *Giant bubble shaped rocks in the flow of the Hornaday River.*

Two hikers descend into the river valley. Coal seams in the steep banks of the lower Hornaday River blacken the slopes. Ten days after being dropped by float plane in Tuktut Nogait National Park, our group of five people hiked into the settlement of Paulatuk on the shore of the Beaufort Sea.

The serene beauty of sunlight and shadows draws adventurers out into the frozen environment of the subarctic winter. Despite the long cold winter, water remains open at Cassette Rapids on the Slave River and sends mist into the air. The mist then settles as frost on the nearby trees.

Our Forgotten North: A Glimpse of the Subarctic in Canada's North

The sensation begins the moment the Cessna 185 detaches itself from the clinging surface of the water and begins to climb into the limitless sky. My umbilical cord to the comfortable world of modern civilization has been severed. The whine of the engine gradually fades as the plane becomes a small dot in the distance, then disappears completely. The sensation is building: anxiety, finality and a sense of emptiness sink deeper and deeper into my body, penetrating my soul, my very existence.

My mother and I are left standing beside our small heap of gear, 450 kilometres from the closest human settlement, with no way to contact the outside world. In 22 days the float plane will meet us at a pre-determined location 320 kilometres down river to take us home from this remote and awe-inspiring wilderness.

My anxiety fades as silence begins to fill my deep emptiness. Warm sun, chilled by a north wind sweeping off the tundra, touches my face. The sweet fragrant smell of Labrador tea blossoms warming in the late morning sun greets my nose. Around me is an incredible expanse of sky and a land sparsely dotted with scrubby clumps of spruce. It all pours into me, through every one of my senses. It is like a rebirth, an awakening to the natural world, a profoundly spiritual and healing experience. I feel complete, content, present in the here and now. I am at one with the natural world, part of the whole.

I think about that. Humans *are* part of the natural world but our industrialized society severs the connection and makes us uncertain of our place. I am relieved to leave behind the detached existence of urban society, that place where we live in our heads but not in our hearts. I am happy to be fulfilled again.

Each time I journey into the wilds of this great land, I feel a sense of reconnection to the earth. "Our Forgotten North" is my way of sharing the subarctic with you, with all humanity, for the sake of humanity. It is a journey of adventure, discovery and spiritual connection to the wild and stunningly beautiful subarctic. Meet the wildlife, the people and the awesome scenery through photographs, personal experiences and natural history.

The Forgotten North is a zone of ecological transition in which thick boreal forests at the northern edge of the treeline gradually dissolve into small clumps of gnarled spruce on the open tundra. The land is filled with unforgettable treasures, many unique in Canada and the world, ranging from the intricate detail of minute yet vibrant pink blossoms of moss campion to the magnificent grandeur of Virginia Falls and dazzling autumn vistas in the Richardson Mountains. The land abounds with wildlife, from prehistoric-looking muskox to elusive wolf, masses of caribou to playfully curious river otter, and delicate yet enduring arctic tern to predatory great horned owl.

Subarctic seasons are distinct and dramatic: long, warm summer days, when dusk turns to dawn and temperatures rise above 30°C; equally long but cold winter nights, when temperatures can fall below -40°C and the skies are filled with the majestic northern lights, illuminating the darkness with a flurry of spectacular activity. Spring and autumn are brief and exciting, filled with rapid change.

Aboriginal peoples make up the about half of the sparse population. Over centuries, they have developed a way of life that is intimately intertwined with the land and all it supports, a way of life that considers humans a part of nature that must live within and respect natural laws. Aboriginal cultures date back more than 8,000 years, long before the first Europeans arrived in the 1700s.

A muskox stretches after waking from a midday sleep in the Thelon Wildlife Sanctuary. The mainland muskoxen population was nearly hunted to extinction by 1900, but today many thousand animals thrive under protection.

Beginning deep in the boreal forest, the Forgotten North extends from the Slave River rapids, gateway to the north, and Wood Buffalo National Park, through a series of plummeting waterfalls and magnificent river canyons. Then spans the treeline through the Taiga Shield, with its great rock outcrops, wind-blown conifers, rushing rivers and crystal clear lakes, including the immense Great Slave Lake and its cliff-bordered East Arm. The northeast of the Forgotten North is the "place where god began," the last pocket of trees isolated by open tundra that makes up the Thelon Wildlife Sanctuary. Following the Mackenzie drainage north by northwest takes us into the land of majestic mountains and mythical rivers and finally to the disorienting maze of the Mackenzie Delta and the scenic Dempster Highway, the most northerly road link to the south.

The incredibly diverse subarctic is often forgotten when people read and talk about the Canadian north. It is not home to polar bears,

On the Dempster highway, the late evening sun paints the clouds of a dissipating storm.

icebergs or Inuit seal hunters. The Forgotten North is something different, a place most of us know little about. It is isolated and inaccessible, yet more accessible than the high arctic and therefore threatened by development. Although development is so far dwarfed by the vastness of this remote land, there is concern among the people of the Forgotten North. Many cherish the pristine nature of this wild and virtually untouched land, and fear politicians enamoured by "Roads to Resources" will bring a wave of industrial and mining development.

Today, Canadians have the chance to preserve huge tracts of land where plants and wildlife live undisturbed, where nature and ecology play out timeless processes free from human intervention. The Forgotten North is one of the last places on earth with vast expanses of uninhabited land that can still be put aside for enjoyment by all earth's creatures.

Autumn colour flows over the alpine slopes of the Richardson Mountains, just north of the summit on the Dempster Highway.

Autumn displays its colour in the subarctic foliage of poplar, willow, fireweed and high-bush cranberry.

White pelicans spend long summer days bobbing for fish in the calmer rapids of the Slave River. This most northerly colony of white pelicans is the only one in the world that nests on river islands protected by raging whitewater - too dangerous for even the most experienced whitewater kayak enthusiasts or river rafters.

The subarctic is an ecological transition zone filled with an abundance of wildlife, including rare species like the whooping crane, white pelican and wood bison. Populations of these threatened species have recently stabilized and even begun to recover, assisted by special protected areas and the remoteness and undisturbed state of the Forgotten North.

In 1941 there were only 21 whooping cranes left in the world but with the help of dedicated biologists and the preservation of their secluded summer nesting grounds in and around Wood Buffalo National Park, the whooping crane is making a comeback. Today there are 261 of these magnificent birds, with a wild population of 133 nesting in these northerly wetlands and wintering in the Aransas Refuge in Texas. The whooping crane is North America's tallest bird, with a wing span of two metres or more, a standing height of 1.5 metres and a weight of 7.5 kilograms.

Before European settlement, white pelicans nested throughout much of western North America. Conservation efforts were initiated by a sudden, massive decline thought to be caused by widespread use of toxic chemicals. Populations have since rebounded and the white pelican was removed from the endangered species list in 1987. The number of nests on the Slave River near Fort Smith has grown from 25 to over 300 in just twenty years.

Wood bison historically ranged north to Lac la Martre and south to the Rocky Mountain foothills in Colorado. By 1891 fewer than 300 animals remained, mainly in the present day Wood Buffalo National Park. Interbreeding with introduced plains bison increased over all numbers but also brought cattle diseases to the herds. Later a few disease free animals with original wood bison features were relocated further north to the Mackenzie Bison Range, where 1300 bison now live. Another 2700 bison roam the Wood Buffalo area, where human intervention remains a threat. Ranchers are concerned that bison may return the diseases to their now disease-free cattle, although research indicates this is unlikely.

Upper: *The threat display of a common loon defending its territory.*
Lower: *Bunchberry blossoms become brilliant red clusters of berries in late summer and fall. They are also known as dwarf dogwood.*

Wild herds of bison roam free in the Mackenzie Bison Range, the South Nahanni, the Slave River Lowlands, and Wood Buffalo National Park.

Upper: *This pictograph near Fort Smith was strategically left by Crees pursued by Dogribs, who mysteriously abandoned the chase after seeing it.*
Lower: *Moonrise at the float plane base marks the end of a wilderness journey.*

Upper: *Dust lingers after a roll in a wallow. The farther a bison can roll over on his hump, the greater the display of strength to other bulls during the rut.*
Lower: *Paddling with a canine passenger in the late summer midnight sun.*

A wild rose finds nourishment in the decaying foliage and deadfall of seasons past.

The brown, silt-laden Slave River is transformed into an upheaval of whitewater as it tumbles from Fort Fitzgerald to Fort Smith. Four sets of rapids are formed over a 25 kilometre stretch as the Canadian Shield pinches the immense flow of the river, revealing extremes of both beauty and power.

The rapids are the only major obstacle to navigation along the water route between southern Canada and the Arctic Ocean. Most traders chose a long portage around this "gateway to the north" rather than risk losing precious cargo, while natives, early explorers and fur traders used a well-established series of shorter portages down the east side of the river. Modern travelers can follow the historic eastern route through calmer water between islands, down small twisted side channels, and over well-worn portage trails.

Blue-eyed grass, like many boreal flowers, are jewels of vibrant colour, rising up from the thick green mat of the forest floor.

At the edge of the rapids, serenity is attained in a pool of water stranded by the declining level of the Slave River in autumn.

The wild whitewater of the Slave River rapids was a major obstacle to the trappers, traders and natives, who travelled north with supplies and south with furs. The earliest portage routes were well established by the late 1700's and can still be travelled today.

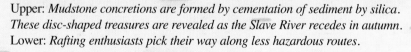

Upper: *Mudstone concretions are formed by cementation of sediment by silica. These disc-shaped treasures are revealed as the Slave River recedes in autumn.*
Lower: *Rafting enthusiasts pick their way along less hazardous routes.*

Upper Left: *The shooting star blooms in early summer.*
Upper Right: *In early June, these eggs will hatch into gull chicks.*
Lower: *Paddling in the midnight sun is like a peaceful dream.*

Upper: *A young river otter demonstrates characteristic curiosity.*
Lower: *Gull chicks spend spring in nests on islands along the Slave River rapids, protected from predators unable to access these island sanctuaries.*

A young great horned owl is surprised by the sight of a fellow visitor to the falls. Although this dominant avian predator possesses a keen sense of hearing, the roar of the falls made it possible for me to approach without detection.

Wind bound camp at the far reaches of the treeline. More valuable than gold, the Thelon Wildlife Sanctuary can be found at the end of this rainbow.

Upper: *Nesting swallows find natural protection from weather and predators in the karst bluffs of the Salt River near Fort Smith.*
Lower: *The midnight sun casts shadows of clustered spruce on the tent door.*

The pasque-flower, or wild crocus, pushes through the chaotic mass of decomposing foliage from autumn past. It is the first flower to emerge after the snow has melted.

Upper: *Bush planes are an important link to the remote wilderness of the north.*
Lower: *Yellow water lily after the rain. An important food source for muskrat and beaver, it can be found in many ponds, shallow lakes and sluggish streams.*

Drying fish at a Dene camp. Preparation of the fish includes meticulous cleaning and cutting to facilitate fast, even drying. Sometimes it is smoked over a smudge fire using wood specially selected for smoldering.

The Dene people have a long history of living on the land. Today they continue to harvest caribou, moose, beaver, fish and birds for food and clothing, as well as berries, mint, rat root, chamomile and birch bark for food, medicinal remedies and other useful items.

Hides are tanned using a traditional process that produces a more durable, stronger, lighter and warmer material than commercially tanned hides. Both sides of the hide are scraped to remove flesh and hair, and to thin the hide. The hide is soaked in an oily substance, such as brains, then smoked and worked to break down the fibers and soften the material. The process is physically laborious, with each of the steps taking days to complete.

Food and products made from natural sources have an inherent spiritual value and are considered to be of higher quality and durability.

Out on the land, elders use a bed of dwarf birch leaves to lay a midday meal of dry fish, bannock and tea.

Upper: *Hung fish from the fall run are used in winter to feed sled dogs.*
Lower: *Birch bark, porcupine quills and tanned hides and fur are used to make mittens, moccasins, berry baskets and other items.*

Maintaining ancient tradition, Dene drummers tighten the hides on their drums over the camp fire and summon the power of the ancestral spirit.

Upper: *Dene drums are made with birch wood, caribou hide, and sinew.*
Lower: *Crafted from home-tanned moose hide, these moccasins are far more durable than products made from commercially tanned hides.*

Drumming initiates a spiritual connection between the Dene and the Creator during a celebration, healing circle or sweat lodge, or the commemoration of a death and subsequent journey to the next world. Together with song, drumming is essentially a form of prayer. Special events and meetings are opened by prayer, and early morning drumming and singing put the Creator ahead of everything else.

The drum is a spiritual tool and must be respected and handled accordingly. Its keeper must follow spiritual laws and live an undefiled life. During a drum dance, spirituality is sensed by all. The beat of the drum and the chant of the song inspire people to get up and join the dancing circle.

The songs of the drum dance are also for entertainment and amusement during journeys out on the land.

My approach distracts a red fox from digging up her food cache. I surprised the animal with her face buried in the snow sniffing out the goods. Her thick coat is evidence of a winter abundant in good food sources.

For a few short weeks, trembling aspen shimmer brilliant oranges and yellows in the autumn winds, like many tambourines.

An aerial view of the Salt Plains reveals the shape of islands of salt-stressed spruce casting their evening shadows on the mud flats, where the soil is too saline and bare for plant life to grow.

Upper: *Wildlife tracks, like these of the sandhill crane, add to the patterns of cracks and eroded boulders littering the mud flats of Grosbeak Lake.*
Lower: *Texture and scale in the mud near the end of a long dry summer.*

Bears, wolves, moose and bison are among the large mammals attracted to the salt deposits to lick this mineral so vital to their diet.

The ever-changing environment of Grosbeak Lake near Fort Smith displays precipitated salt after a long dry spell. Salt accelerates the erosion of the erratics, boulders left behind by glaciers. Together with years of freeze-thaw action, this process breaks down the weaker layers and pockets to create wonderfully weird shapes. Granular in texture, the granite boulders display contorted surfaces, sweeping grooves, gaping hollows, gouges and deep cavities.

Salt water has flowed onto the Salt Plains for thousands of years, creating an unusual vegetation community. Salt tolerant and salt resistant plants have evolved over time, lining the edges of mud flats and establishing vegetation islands of salt-stressed spruce. The bare mud flats themselves are too saline to support vegetation.

The salt was originally left behind when vast ancient seas dried up 270 million years ago. Thousands of feet of sedimentary rock cover the salt beds in other parts of the prairies but here they are much closer to the surface. Groundwater flows through the subterranean salt beds and is then forced upward by the bedrock of the Interior Plains butting against the granite of the Canadian Shield. Once at the surface, the water evaporates in the summer heat. Some salt is left in crystalline mounds at the outflow of springs, while the rest is distributed across the plains and into nearby waterways.

The Slavey, Beaver, Chipewyan, and Cree people have harvested crystalline salt from the plains for hundreds of years. Salt was gathered, pounded and used to preserve fish, waterfowl and wild game. Following the arrival of the Hudson's Bay Company and the Northwest Company, salt was distributed throughout the Mackenzie basin by a network of trading posts and missions. In the early 1900s, up to two tonnes of salt were gathered annually.

The Salt Plains form a truly unusual natural environment that invites the adventurous to visit during any of the four seasons. Unique in Canada, the plains are preserved as part of Wood Buffalo National Park, itself a World Heritage Site.

Upper: *After days of rain, much of the Salt Plains rest under water. Salt deposits are dissolved and transported into the waterways.*
Lower: *A natural spring bubbles to the earth's surface. This water is so heavily saturated, salt precipitates even under the water.*

Soft mud oozes up to my knees as I gaze out over the Salt Plains, trying to get a true sense of the place. Bright red samphire and golden yellow Nuttall's meadow grass line the alternating mud flats. Patches of dwarf birch, yellow and orange from the first frost, add relief to the foreground, while clusters of spruce punctuate the skyline. Fluffy white clouds reflect off the placid, shallow waters, as sandpiper calls pierce the silence.

In another stretch of the plains, Grosbeak Lake comprises the muddy remnants of a once-large lake, and adds its unique features to the salty landscape. Cracks in the drying mud and lines of salt precipitate create a jigsaw puzzle pattern, criss-crossed by the tracks of birds, animals and humans. The mud flats are dotted with glacial erratics eroded into bizarre and fantastic shapes by salt and freezing temperatures. Hundreds of gulls nest at the centre of the lake, protected by water and deep mud.

A view of the Salt Plains from the top of the escarpment. Salt-tolerant plants like red samphire border the mud flats, followed by salt-resistant plants like Nuttall's salt-meadow grass.

Scoured by glaciers that retreated about 10,000 years ago, the smooth surface of a rock outcrop in the Precambrian shield reflects the midnight sun.

Some of the oldest rock in the world is found in the taiga shield, exposed as giant precambrian outcrops worn smooth by erosion, or as monolithic bluffs where peregrine falcons and eagles nest. Innumerable lakes nestle in glacially-carved depressions, connected by a maze of rushing rivers and streams. Long sinuous eskers break up the landscape. The uplands, with dry sparse soils, are interspersed by pockets of wetlands and open forests, as well as shrub-lands and meadows more common in the tundra. Caribou lichen and moss cling to rock surfaces bearing a thin dusting of soil.

More than fifty species of mammals live in the taiga shield - the transition zone between forest and tundra - including moose, wolf, fox, beaver, lynx, black bear and the migratory barrenground caribou. Hundreds of thousands of birds come to nest or feed on their way to tundra breeding grounds. Unfortunately, this vast tract of wilderness is also rich in diamonds and other minerals and is attracting considerable exploration and development.

Monolithic rock bluffs plummet into the Taltson River in shield country. Evidence of higher water levels in the past can be clearly seen at the base of the rock wall.

Upper: *Erractics are left behind by the retreat of the Laurentide Ice Sheet.* Lower: *Edible crowberry contrasts eroded viens in the striated rock of shield country.*

At Lac du Rocher, small clumps of trees are very sparsely scattered among the granite outcrops of the Candaian Shield. At about 180 km east of Yellowknife, Lac du Rocher, at the edge of treeline, is a pristine setting for the beautiful lines of a cedar strip canoe.

Upper: *A canoeing paradise in the subarctic wilderness of the taiga shield.*
Lower: *Hiking an esker is bug free and easy walking. Chances for seeing wildlife are good for the same reasons.*

Labrador tea creates a striking contrast against red algae.

An icy bay on the Slave River near Fort Smith. Despite consecutive days of temperatures below -30°C, the dynamic energy of the river and the turbulence of the rapids keeps the water in this bay open throughout winter. Mist rises from the surface of the open water into the cold winter air, creating clouds of fog that drift above the forested river banks.

Upper: *Most of the barrenground caribou herds winter inside the treeline.*
Lower: *Nature's ornaments formed by the ebb and flow of the river.*

The top layer of the snow pack is sculpted by wind. The strengths of various layers are affected by pressures and temperatures in the snow pack and the air temperature during initial precipitation.

The beauty of an ice-laden trapper's cabin is also an indication of poor insulation. Although snow has excellent insulating properties, heat from inside transforms the snow to ice, which is a very poor insulator. This is why snow shelters are for temporary use and need to be rebuilt regularly.

The low angle of the winter sun creates a landscape of enchanting reflections, deep shadows and refracted beams as it bounces off crystals of ice and snow. Reflected sunlight bathes the surroundings in bright light, while beams shoot upward from the ice, and ice-coated branches are back-lit by the sun.

As the sun nears the horizon, an array of warm hues fills the sky. A profusion of pink and purple or orange and yellow tones silhouette scrubby spruce, thick boreal forest, smooth undulating shield rock, or wide frozen lakes and rivers.

With a wide range of colours, skylines, cloud formations and light phenomena, no two sunsets are alike in the Forgotten North.

Upper: *In the late afternoon sunset of early winter, the open water of Kakisa Lake dusts the bare deciduous branches with hoar frost.*
Lower: *Winter nights come alive with the aurora borealis dancing overhead.*

A teepee is blessed by one of the most spectacular natural phenomena on earth. Watching an auroral display is like watching a great spirit capriciously painting the dark sky with electric green light. Huge swaths and fine filaments can be intense at the onset, then fade quickly or sometimes linger.

In Dogrib legend, Ithenhiela fled on a caribou that used magic to throw obstacles in the path of a relentless pursuer. The caribou created hills from a lump of earth, muskeg from a patch of moss, forest from a branch and the Rocky Mountains from a stone. At the end of their journey, Ithenhiela pulled a forbidden arrow from a tree and was carried to the sky, where he has lived ever since. The aurora that appears in the northern sky is Ithenhiela's fingers moving about.

Scientists believe the northern lights are created by electrically charged particles carried by solar winds. When the charged particles pass by the earth, some enter the earth's magnetic field and are guided toward the polar regions. There the particles interact with gases present in the atmosphere and release energy that is seen as the glow of the northern lights.

Whatever one believes, the northern lights are a compensating splendour in the long, cold winters of the Forgotten North. Lights fill the dark night like capricious flames of raging fire sprawling across the sky, moving with the speed of light and the flow of a whimsical ballerina. Countless particles move as if brilliantly choreographed, dancing in an ever-changing symphony of light and color. Cold and darkness fade away as the lights lift the soul and rekindle the spirit.

The play of light in the subarctic sky also occurs during the day. Sun dogs, sun pillars and halos occur when sunlight passes through ice fog at altitudes of 5,000 to 15,000 metres, with billions of crystals acting like tiny prisms, refracting and reflecting sunlight. Sun pillars usually occur in extremely cold air at sunrise and sunset when a beam of sunlight reflects off the bottom of plate shaped crystals with angular edges. Sun dogs are created when sunlight enters the sides of plate crystals and is refracted twice inside.

Upper: *Sundogs appear in the late afternoon of a cold winter day.*
Lower: *A sun pillar emerges from the horizon, piercing the cloud cover.*

The scarlet aurora borealis is a rare phenomenon that last occurred on the night of March 23, 1991. Experts say the unusual color is caused by powerful solar winds hitting the earth's magnetic field and causing a "great magnetic storm." The winds, moving in excess of 1000 kilometres per second, are in turn caused by an unusually massive solar flare.

Capturing the northern lights on film takes a combination of luck and experience. The essentials are a manual camera with a tripod, a fast film and a night sky with a vivid aurora. Then the photographer has to guess how bright the aurora are and how long to hold the shutter open. Often the photographs have white flecks in them. These are bright stars that move during long film exposures.

The unusual color and awesome expanse of the rare red aurora is momentous enough for some to believe it was caused by a huge explosion or fire, or that the world was coming to an end.

Depending on temperature, weather and timing, the short autumn can be colourful, vibrant and warm one year, and dreary, wet and bone-chilling the next.

The setting sun illuminates the gnarled outline of ice-coated branches, where willow forests sprawl among the moister areas of the boreal forest. These areas are prime habitat for moose, which feed on the young buds and tender shoots.

The twisted silhouette of a white birch contrasts with the rigid landscape of the Canadian Shield. The flexible, waterproof bark was traditionally used for making canoes, baskets and other containers.

Contrary to southern perceptions, summer in the Forgotten North is usually very dry and warm, with temperatures often above 30°C. Days can last 19 to 24 hours at their peak, depending on latitude, giving subarctic vegetation an essential period of accelerated growth. Silently paddling a canoe through these seemingly never-ending hours of dusk-turning-to-dawn is a spiritual experience.

The people of this land are busiest during the long days of summer, making maximal use of the extended daylight. People travel out on the land, gather and prepare foodstuffs for the inevitable winter, and simply reconnect with the land. Sleep becomes a low priority, purely a consequence of physical need.

Autumn can be intensely beautiful and dramatically short, with orange, red, and yellow running rampant through the mixed forests, busy understory and open ground. Each year is different, depending on when the first frost comes, how severe it is and how long it stays. Small changes in weather patterns can have an enormous impact on this brief, fickle, subarctic season.

Winter is long and cold, but it is a welcome season for many people, a time to rest a weary body after the busy summer days, to hibernate and to reconnect with extended family and friends. It is also a time of magical beauty and extraordinary light, as the aurora dances for hours in the night sky.

Spring is eagerly anticipated and always welcome, lifting the spirits of the people and beckoning them out into the warmer but still sub-zero temperatures. By March, each day can be 8 minutes longer than the last and soon the snow is melting and giving way to an explosion of growth. Tight buds burst into vibrant green leaves in only a few days, as the land awakens to a new year.

The serenity of this scene is thwarted in reality by the constant buzz of hungry insects bouncing off the bug netting. Sunset is a prime time for these tiny beasts because the heat of the midday has subsided and the wind has vanished.

Upper: *Autumn signals impending repose for much of nature.*
Lower: *A duckling at dusk without the protection and guidance if its mother is easy quarry for predators.*

Typical of rivers in the Forgotten North, break-up on the Hay River sends huge slabs of ice onto the banks, where they slowly melt in the warming sun to form candled ice.

Upper: *In spring, the massive expanse of ice on Great Slave Lake creates heavy fog over the warmer landscape at its shores.*
Lower: *Candled ice tinkles and chimes as it falls from slabs of river ice.*

The sun is low in the sky during the daylight hours of winter, casting long, dark shadows across the untouched snow. The striped patterns and the subtle tones of grey have a calming effect in the deep quiet of winter.

A long time ago, an old woman asked her people for a meal of beaver blood but times were hard and they could not provide it. In despair, she sat down by a falls and was swept away in the current, never to be seen again. The spirit of the woman returned as a rainbow that watches over the falls to this day.

Places of danger are often associated with stories such as this, reminding people to ask for help and guidance from their powerful Creator. At Alexandra Falls the spirits of an old man and woman care for the waters. People make offerings of tobacco, matches, tea or bullets at the falls and pray for help in leading a good life. If a rainbow appears, the spirits are looking kindly on you. If a rainbow does not appear, the spirits are unhappy and something bad might happen.

Upper: *An old woman's spirit appears as a rainbow in the mist of the falls.* Lower: *In the depths of the caverns, a goddess figure is created as the sun casts dark shadows on the towering limestone walls of the Hay River Gorge.*

A thin ledge of disintegrated rock and organic remains has enough nutrients to support a small ecosystem between the river's edge and the canyon walls.

As I walk along the Twin Falls Trail, I can hear the intense roar of Alexandra Falls dropping 36 metres over a precipitous limestone cliff into the Hay River Gorge. Hearing the falls before seeing them, enhances one's comprehension of the sheer volume of the water and the power that can be created by nature.

From Louise Falls to Alexandra Falls, the three kilometre Twin Falls trail winds its way through distinct pockets of jack pine, spruce, and mixed forest of white spruce and trembling aspen.

A 36-metre drop over the limestone ledge at Alexandra Falls marks the beginning of the spectacular Hay River gorge. This 25-kilometre stretch of water flows between golden walls up to 50 metres high and through ancient geological formations as beautiful as they are unique. At the 2-kilometre mark, the calm river is interrupted by a further 16-metre drop at Louise Falls.

Limestone cliffs along the route are gradually crumbling under the onslaught of time and erosion. Tall columns of limestone have calved from the sides, many topped with a patch of forest that has slowly adjusted to the changing angle of the earthen surface on the fragile pillar. High up on the gorge walls, tree trunks are literally splitting in half as new slabs of limestone slowly break away from the cliffs. Deep caverns and crevasses cast bright light and dark shadows on the cliff walls. Scree slopes lie heaped against the base of the walls.

The Hay River basin contains no natural storage, so runoff patterns show great seasonal variation. In spring, huge volumes of water crash over the edge of the limestone shelves. At times, a thick mist rises into the air, welling up from the base of the falls and filling the gorge before dissipating over the treetops. By the end of a very dry summer, the falls have dwindled into dozens of tiny rivulets, highlighting the finer notches in the limestone ledges.

The first long icicles form on the sides of Alexandra Falls in early winter and gradually, as temperatures drop, the falls freeze over, until the remaining flow thunders off the ledge and into a hole in a mound of ice. Mist from this last stream of open water floats into the air and gathers at the top of the falls, forming a peak like a shark's snout rising from the water, its jagged jaws of icicles outlining its open steaming throat.

Upper: *Curiosity overcomes the fear of a river otter surprised by the sight of a visitor it cannot hear over the roar of the rapids.*
Lower: *Louise Falls transforms into cascading rivulets after a long dry summer.*

Pure stands of trembling aspen can be found in the rich, fertile soils of moist depressions. Considered a weather indicator by some, leaves shimmering in the absence of any perceptible wind signal a storm is on its way.

Upper: *A ruffed grouse chick has not yet mastered the skill of flight.*
Lower Left: *Bluebells add a splash of purplish blue to rocky terrain.*
Lower Right: *At Louise Falls, ancient fossils can be found near the bluffs.*

The second of two falls on Escarpment Creek cascades over the predominantly limestone and shale cliffs that record 450 million years of geological history. Northern sweet vetch, or wild sweet pea, adorns a talus slope that tumbles into the amphitheater-shaped basin of the falls .

Upper: *Trappers' cabins dot the wilderness within the treeline.*
Lower: *Lichen clings to a small protrusion in the bark of a birch tree.*

Early in the winter, water still flows at Escarpment Creek, creating a frozen world of fantastical ice formations.

The fishbowl-shaped canyon of the second falls appears before us as a fabulous world of white, a fantasia of free flowing water spilling over frozen mounds of stepped cascades. Spray splatters from the rushing water and mist floats into the crisp, cold air. We feel the tingling chill on our faces as we venture into the depths of this winter wonderland, first to the back of the fishbowl beneath the overhanging falls, then down the canyon, following the creek as it flows beneath the ice.

Variations in cold northern temperatures cause moisture to form different crystalline structures, creating a multitude of uniquely artistic ice formations in the canyon of Escarpment Creek. Mist deposited on the back wall beneath the overhanging falls forms long, thick stalactite features that look like matted sheep's tails. Further downstream, meringue-like pillars of frozen froth emerge from openings where turbulent water has kept the ice at bay. They are formed as froth rises in the cold air, freezes and is in turn pushed up by more froth, building pillars up to a metre high on the creek's icy surface.

Throughout the winter, various stages of freeze-up occur at the waterfalls on Escarpment Creek, as well as most of the other falls along the geological formation known as the Alexandra Escarpment. The process usually starts in November and by spring most of the falls have become frozen cascades of solid ice.

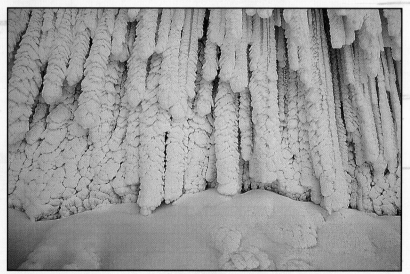

Upper: *A frozen mound of stepped cascades builds under the falling water.*
Lower: *Spray and mist from the falling water freezes onto the overhanging limestone cliff, like a wall of long, matted sheep's tails.*

At Lady Evelyn Falls on the Kakisa River, grandiose ice falls appear on the side wall in winter, where only insignificant trickles of water can be found in spring and summer.

Upper: *The autumn colours of balsam poplar, willow and trembling aspen leaves litter the ground for a short time before the first snow falls.*
Lower: *High-bush cranberry, or mooseberry, makes delectable jams and jellies.*

An observer provides a true sense of scale against the grandeur of Wallace Creek's last drop over the escarpment.

The day after the fire, sweeping lines emphasizing the lay of the land can be seen in the pattern of the burn.

Upper: *The degree of disturbance from the last burn is revealed in the vegetation patterns of the regenerating forest.*
Lower: *A few lonely jackpine stand among the regrowth from deciduous roots.*

The Dene traditionally had a thorough understanding of natural factors affecting fires. In the past, they set controlled fires in specific locations to encourage the kinds of animals and edible plants they liked to harvest.

Fire is essential to the natural succession of boreal forest, with most areas burning about once every 100 years, changing the nature of the forest floor and making way for regeneration. Natural fires leave patchy disturbance patterns and a variety of organic debris. Some fires are very hot, opening the cones of jackpine and releasing the seeds. Other fires burn at lower temperatures, allowing deciduous trees to grow back from roots left in the ground.

Despite claims to the contrary, current logging practices do not approximate the complex processes of natural forest fires.

Forest fires are left to run their natural course unless human assets are threatened. The CL-215 is the world's only aircraft designed as a water-scooping bomber and can scoop 5000 litres in 10 seconds, dropping it over a fire in only one second.

Intensely coloured sunsets are created when heavy smoke from forest fires fills the air. Often smoke is so dense that even the midday sun is filtered and transformed into an orange ball.

The spectacular waterfalls cascading off the series of escarpments along the south side of the upper Mackenzie River, between the Hay River and the Trout River, are the result of ancient geological activity on a continental scale. In pre-glacial times, about 2 million years ago, major drainages in this region flowed east toward Hudson Bay, completely opposite to the flow of the modern upper Mackenzie River. These pre-glacial rivers cut through hundreds of metres of older sedimentary rock and widened the ancient valleys. The nature of sedimentary rock strata varies greatly. Weaker layers offer little resistance to erosion, resulting in rapid widening of the valley. More resistant layers are less easily eroded, producing escarpments within the broad valley system.

The situation gradually changed as the Laurentide Ice Sheet advanced westward from plateaus near Hudson Bay, blocking the east-flowing rivers and forcing them to find alternate routes. The ice ultimately reached the Mackenzie Mountains and re-directed all drainage north to the Beaufort Sea. The modern Mackenzie River was established as the ice sheet retreated, making the Mackenzie one of the world's largest glacially-implaced drainage systems.

Today, tributaries of the Mackenzie River, including the Hay River, Trout River, Wallace Creek, McNallie Creek and Escarpment Creek, all run north, generally perpendicular to the old drainage valley and its escarpments, inevitably forming numerous waterfalls.

Layers that make up the escarpments, deposited by ancient seas some 460 million years ago, vary in thickness and hardness. Relentless water erosion has worn weaker layers and left more resistant ones, giving each waterfall a unique configuration.

Upper: *Lofty trembling aspen flourish in the rich soils of the boreal forest.*
Lower: *Aspen are a favourite food for beaver. Where aspen is abundant, litters are large.*

Upper Left: *Dragonflies eat insects all summer long and die before autumn.*
Upper Right: *Potentilla survives in the layers of fossils at Sambah Deh Falls.*
Lower: *The raging shoot of Samba Deh Falls on the Trout River.*

Still groggy from winter hibernation, this bear showed its youthfulness in curious, unalarmed behaviour. In a seemingly playful gesture, he nibbled at the dry dead weed in front of him.

Contrary to popular belief, porcupine do not throw their quills. In the face of a perceived threat, they swiftly twist their bodies and flick their tails, jabbing their barbed quills in defense.

Upper: *The bare Trout River canyon is stripped of soil deposits at high water.* Lower: *A variety of rock compositions and structures create distinctly different configurations of rock and water along the Trout River canyon.*

Low water at the upper falls of the Trout River spills out of eroded basins and hollows and over the ledge. The aggregate of the shelf fractures easily into small round fragments, creating smoother, more rounded features and contours.

Downstream from Samba Deh Falls, the Trout River canyon can be accessed through a deep narrow crevasse that culminates in this hidden Shangri-La deep within the canyon walls.

A bull caribou poses majestically, with his stark, white "bell" blowing in the north wind. Caribou migrate from the barrenlands back into the treeline in autumn.

Well-worn paths in the blanket of vegetation, sun bleached antlers, lichen tufts chewed down to the ground, and this back bone are all signs of caribou migration.

Upper: *A caribou trail cuts through a patch of forest on the crest of an esker.*
Lower: *The growth of the tundra vegetation shows that this antler must have been resting here for years.*

It is the final day of our three week journey down the Thelon River and we have seen only a single one of the thousands, or even hundreds of thousands, of caribou that usually migrate through this area. Engrossed in thought, I wander around the archeological site surrounding our camp, stepping over stones that once circled the caribou hide tents of inland Inuit. Sun-bleached bone fragments and small rock chips lie scattered about, left behind in the tool-making process. I think about the harsh life these people must have lead.

A low, repetitive noise distracts me from my thoughts. Probably a goose, I think... or maybe a few geese or... what is that noise? I look up and across the river to the opposite bank. There are too many caribou to count. Larger ones, smaller ones, frisky little calves, coated in light beige, white or rusty brown. Grunts, snorts and clicks fill my ears from a thousand animals. They are the most intense sounds I have heard during our trip. It is like nothing I could have imagined.

The Chipewyan say that "no one knows the way of the wind and the caribou." Meat, blood and stomach contents from these animals traditionally provided a balanced diet for native people. Antler, bone and sinew were used to make tools, weapons and ornaments. Skins were used for tents, bedding and clothing. Even the nomadic movement of the people was guided by the seasonal migration of the caribou. The migratory whims of the caribou no longer mean life or death but caribou retain significant economic value and spiritual importance to the people of the Forgotten North.

When humans approach, the gregarious caribou run a short distance, then stop and turn for another look, their heads perky and their soft white muzzles pointing. Then they trot jauntily away, dismissing the threat. One winter I dressed in a white sheet and tried to sneak up on a small herd but they were not fooled. Four individuals pranced back and forth in front of me, as if to see if I would chase them, then wandered off unconcerned.

The synchronized gait of caribou gracefully prancing across Thekulthili Lake near the Taltson River in shield country sends a distinct clicking sound into the crisp cold air. This characteristic sound is caused by tendons slipping over the sesamoid bone in their feet as they walk.

A rough-legged hawk circles and cries 'keeer' over its cliff-side nest as a canoe passes under wing.

Upper: *A huge population of geese molt over several weeks in the Thelon Oasis.*
Lower: *Stratified with weaker layers, rocks are eroded into uniform patterns by trapped moisture and freeze-thaw action.*

An esker left behind by the Laurentide Ice Sheet some 9,000 years ago stands in stark contrast to a pocket of the boreal forest. This pocket, set in a sea of barren tundra, makes the Thelon Wildlife Sanctuary unique.

A cliff top view of the crystal-clear water of a Thelon River tributary.

Elders refer to it as "the place where god began when the world was created." Thousands of muskoxen roam free, wolves live their lives without learning to fear humans and hundreds of thousands of caribou migrate to secluded calving grounds in the vast wilderness. Countless geese and swans molt and nest, while peregrine falcons, rough-legged hawks and gyrfalcons raise their young on sheer cliffs that fall away to the clear blue waters of the Thelon River. Barrenland grizzlies roam supreme, while arctic ground squirrels, known as sic-sics, cavort close to their dens.

In the Thelon Wildlife Sanctuary, I become a member of the wildlife population, just another creature living in the wilderness. One day I follow a wolf who is fully aware of my presence. She pauses to listen at a willow shrub, then pounces and sends a ptarmigan bursting forth in a flurry of excitement. Next she saunters along a gully, stops about 10 metres away, observes me for a minute or two, then casually goes about her business. There is no fear and no aggression, just plain curiosity.

I know from the scent that muskoxen are near. They will let me approach in plain view but if I hide behind shrubs and sneak up on them, they flee in a cloud of dust and thundering hooves.

One day my mother and I sight a moose fleeing into thick willows, and she decides to try and flush him out. A rustling sound emanates from the willows. "What are you doing in here?" she asks, somewhat surprised. "I'm not in there," I reply, trying to get a better look. I climb onto a mound of sand to find a set of soft velvety horns peeking out over the ratty willow tops. The moose studies me for a while, then flees as my mother emerges from the willows with a big goose in her arms, its head buried in her elbow as if trying to hide.

Despite the abundance of wildlife, nature has its own ideas, as John Hornby and his party discovered in 1927. They had planned to winter on the Thelon but starved to death because they failed to consider migratory patterns of the caribou.

A pink splash of alpine azalea blossoms hugs a lichen-covered boulder. The minute leathery leaves of this matted dwarf shrub are coated by a waxy substance that reduces water loss in the dry tundra climate. The first flower to bloom on the barrenlands in spring, it can be found exposed to the sun beside patches of melting snow.

The start of a wilderness expedition. Float planes drop off adventurers and their supplies far out in the tundra, at the edge of the Thelon Wildlife Sanctuary.

Upper: *Muskoxen like to feed on new growth of willow, leaving qiviut, their soft under hair, snagged on branches and blowing in the tundra breeze.*
Lower: *A rough-legged hawk's nest on a cliff over the Hanbury River.*

Hand crafted by an ancestor of the present-day Dene, this arrowhead or spear tip from the late Taltheilei period could be a thousand years old. The side notching feature of this artifact dates back to as early as 800 A.D.

Upper: *Moss campion grows in tight mats of tiny leaves and flowers, deeply anchored by its tap-root and pressed over rock and sand.*
Lower: *A gyrfalcon chick, a member of the largest falcon species in the world.*

Upper: *The agile, graceful arctic tern is the longest migrator in the world.*
Lower: *Mountain avens rotate to face the sun 24 hours a day, making the most of the short northern summers.*

The river at Beverly Lake has left the farthest reaches of the treeline and flows out into the barrenlands. This area was a meeting place of the Inuit and Chipewyan, as they followed the barrenground caribou to the calving grounds just north of the Lake. Ironically it wasn't until the last day of our 22-day journey, while among the archeological remnants of one of these ancient hunting camps, that we saw our first and only caribou herd.

A rock cairn on a knoll above Parry Falls is surrounded by scrubby spruce adorned with colourful fragments of cloth, left as offerings by those who have come to experience the healing power of the waters. The spiritual ambiance is enhanced by a campfire puffing smoke into the air.

Every year in early August, Dene from all over the region make a pilgrimage to this sacred site, a place of awesome natural power, rich with cultural and spiritual significance. Here they make offerings and ask the spirit of the old woman who watches over the falls to help them lead a good and healthy life.

Those who need healing stay at the falls for a night or two, while the others camp at the lake nearby, praying that those remaining at the falls receive what they ask. Dene youth come to learn the traditional ways, to gain knowledge of the land and to hear the stories of their people, their elders and their ancestors.

The flow of the Lockhart River is bent in two places by a spectacular configuration of sheer cliffs, giving rise to the 42-metre drop at Parry Falls. The congregation on the rock knoll at the top of the falls provides a striking sense of scale.

This elder travelled hundreds of kilometres by plane, boat and trail to reach Parry Falls, where she will drink from the healing waters and participate in a healing ceremony.

A tight clump of saxifrage, which in Latin means "rock breaker," spills over the incline like a natural rockery garden, rooting itself in crevices bulging with soil and organic remains. The succulent basal leaves, in the form of rosettes, turn orange and red after the shock of the first frost.

Redcliff Island, The Gap, Fortress Island and McDonald Cliff are part of an extensive series of breath-taking formations along the East Arm of Great Slave Lake. In sharp contrast to the adjacent rugged glaciated granite and gneiss country, the folded sedimentaries and volcanics of the East Arm produce a landscape of gentle slopes that end in dramatic drops into the water, like the 225-metre cliff on Etthen Island. The central part of the East Arm includes Christie Bay, where extraordinarily clear water descends over 600 metres, making it the deepest fresh water in North America.

Located at the edge of the barrenlands, the unique ecological transition zone surrounding the East Arm includes thick boreal forest and expanses of rock, which give way to tundra within tens of kilometres of the lake. This area is being considered for a national park.

Upper: *Where there is little contact with humans, wolves express their curious nature without aggression or fear.*
Lower: *Alpine bearberry splashes the tundra and forest floor with red.*

In the East Arm, many of the shorelines are sheer rock cliffs that plummet into the depths of Great Slave Lake. At 614 metres, it is the deepest lake in Canada.

The cliffs of the Douglas Peninsula provide calm waters in a small inlet of Wildbread Bay, on the East Arm of Great Slave Lake.

This is the original southern boundary of the Thelon Game Sanctuary, created in 1927 for the protection of muskoxen and barrenground caribou. The boundary was moved farther north in 1956 due to mining interests in the area . Today, the fate of the Thelon Wildlife Sanctuary rests in the hands of the Dene and Inuit who both have a stake in its management.

A flight over the "treeline" reveals a zone of gradual ecological transition rather than a precise demarcation. Initially, spaces begin to appear among the trees, exposing fields of mint green lichen interspersed by patches of exposed sand left behind by glacial streams about 9,000 years ago.

Eskers rise above the vast flatland, providing low relief as they wind their way like serpents through the landscape, forming beautiful sandy beaches on the shores of numerous lakes.

Trees become fewer in number and shorter in stature until only a few small, gnarled trees hang on in isolated clumps. Then they too defer to the endless barrenland tundra, with its riddled maze of lakes, rivers, polygons, boulder fields, rock outcrops and occasional sprawling eskers.

In biological terms, the "treeline" is the edge of the continuous forest that delineates the subartic from the tundra community.

Crossing the treeline by air verifies a dwindling forest. The exposed sand of the esker can be seen in patches on the sprawling mat of lichen.

The previous year's fronds of the fragrant shield fern dry out and curl up at the base of the plant, forming a protective layer against erosion and moisture loss.

Upper: *The Franklin Mountains loom majestically over the breadth of the Mackenzie valley along the road to Wrigley.*
Lower: *An immature eagle has not yet fledged and left the nest.*

Death by natural causes, including predation, is both a reality and a necessity because it preserves the balance of the remote wilderness ecosystem. This wolf died of unknown causes.

The immensity of the Mackenzie River and its tributaries is almost unfathomable. Together they drain a basin covering 1.8 million square kilometres and stretching 4,241 kilometres from its uppermost reaches to the Beaufort Sea. It ranks seventh in the world in terms of flow, behind only the Mississippi and the Amazon in the western hemisphere.

Southwest of the basin lie the Mackenzie Mountains, rich with natural treasures: the Ram Plateau, with its majestic karst valleys that drop vertically from broad plateaus; the Cirque of the Unclimbables, batholithic protrusions that pierce the heavens; and the Nahanni, river of myth and magic. Serious adventurers can follow the Canol Trail through deep canyons, rugged mountains, and alpine tundra from the Northwest Territories to the Yukon, via Macmillan Pass.

Upper: *At their confluence, the silt-laden waters of the Liard River contrast with the black waters of the Pettitot, at the edge of the settlement of Fort Liard.*
Lower: *The Liard Range of the Mackenzie Mountains provides a grand backdrop for this Liard valley autumn vista.*

Sheer rock bluffs interrupt the flow of the Nahanni River, bending it 90 degrees and giving rise to the challenging whitewater of the Figure 8 Rapids, also known as Hell's Gate. This calm eddy is created in its wake, allowing paddlers to regroup and regain their composure.

Upper Left: *The cliffs of the Cirque of the Unclimbables harbour glacial lakes.*
Upper Right: *A gastropod embedded in the giant slabs of Sluice Box Rapids.*
Lower: *Sluice Box Rapids ends in the raging torrent of Virginia Falls.*

The Nahanni River appears as a faint silver ribbon through the mist below. Spectacular views are bestowed on hikers who scale the lofty heights of mountain summits along the river valley.

The Nahanni River explodes, sending spray and mist into the air as it crashes into Mason Rock, which divides the cataclysmic waters of Virginia Falls. The entire drop of the falls, a total of 117 metres from Sluice Box Rapids into Five Mile Canyon, is twice the height of Niagara Falls.

We awake on a brisk morning late in August to find the landscape under a heavy, wet blanket of white, the first snowfall of the year on the shores of the Nahanni River. Even the extra gear we packed just in case of snow does little to protect us from the bitterly cold wind blowing up the river corridor. Our wet hands become numb from exposure as we paddle, making the late summer trip almost unbearable.

Despite the inhospitable cold, the fresh snow adds a nuance of alluring beauty to the already dramatic scenery, accentuating the folds, stratifications and other features of the massive mountains along the river valley, and giving depth to the layers of forest rising into the distance. Changing temperatures form brooding mists that rise from the valley floor. Then the sun emerges from behind dark clouds and we rejoice as golden sunlight illuminates the sheer walls of the canyon.

There is magic in the Nahanni and all it embraces. Dusty beige carbonate tuffa mounds emerge from the dark boreal forest, the majestic Ragged Range with the Cirque of the Unclimbables juts into the sky and steamy hot springs beckon the weary traveller. Virginia Falls is one of North America's wonders, its raging water split in half by a giant pillar, then crashing into the canyon below.

On one 50-kilometre stretch, the swift, meandering river is guided along by a series of canyons with walls up to 1.5 kilometres high. This unique section of river was formed by the uplift of mountains, concurrent with entrenchment of an already existing flat, meandering waterway. Narrow tributary canyons join the main river via smooth, undulating spillways that leave perfect bathing pools. Caves dot the omnipresent rock walls, holding hidden secrets deep within.

No wonder the myth, magic and mystery of this place has been revered by generations of native people, explorers and prospectors. Today the Nahanni offers a journey of a lifetime, a journey into rugged wilderness and a journey within oneself, reconnecting the spirit to the earth, grounding the heart, body, mind and soul.

In the shadow of the mountain, morning mist rises from the valley floor through a cluster of dying spruce rooted at the edge of a coarsely segregated alluvial fan.

Upper Left: *A ruffed grouse searches for a new territory in the early snow.*

Upper Right: *The Figure 8 Rapids deceptively appear as mere ripples in the river when viewed from the portage trail traversing the heights of the cliff above.*

Lower: *Late August, and the first snow has come early in the Mackenzie Mountains. At higher elevations, features will remain under a blanket of white until spring.*

The view across the Liard River from Blackstone Park is the perfect setting to contemplate the end of a fourteen-day wilderness journey through the wilds of the Nahanni River. Nahanni Butte emerges from the horizon, marking the confluence of the Nahanni and Liard Rivers.

Fine silt carried by melt water from glaciers suspended in Glacier Lake creates the turquoise green colour.

The Nahanni-Ram region outside the national park is an over-looked area. West of Fort Simpson, the Mackenzie Lowlands abruptly give way and the massive buttresses of the Nahanni Range vault out of the flatness of Little Doctor Lake. Beyond are vast plateaus dotted by little groupings of Dall sheep, grand valleys filled with roaring rivers, limestone caves secreting ice sculptures, meadows skirted by vertical bluffs and pristine lakes that nestle like jewels at the foot of a mountain.

The extreme terrain offers world class challenges for rock climbers, like the granite walls of the Cirque of the Unclimbables, where glaciers nest among spiry peaks and feed the turquoise waters of Glacier Lake.

Not long ago a massive landslide blocked the river. Water backed up and wound along the mountains like a lazy boa constrictor but by the next year much of the natural dam had washed away and the river regained some of its former width.

The Cirque of the Unclimbables rise from the tip of Glacier Lake. The vibrant turquoise lake is fed by glaciers hidden in the sheer peaks.

Upper: *The Ram Range offers spectacular hiking with grand vistas.*
Lower: *Sun cascading through the clouds evokes the magic and mystery of the Nahani-Ram region.*

The Nahanni Range springs from the calm surface of Little Doctor Lake. Silhouettes emphasize the Gap which allows the lake to spread beyond the butresses. The prospector Gus Krause, his wife Mary, and their daughter settled on this beach at Little Doctor Lake.

Norman Wells is named after the oil wells that established the town. Finding the oil was easy because it was seeping from the banks of the Mackenzie River. The town started on oil company land, complete with Royal Canadian Mounted Police Post, hospital, church, recreation hall and worker's quarters.

The US Army started building the Canol Pipeline from Norman Wells to Whitehorse in 1942 to service a string of military airports but the pipeline was barely finished when the Second World War ended, the demand for oil fizzled and the pipeline was abandoned.

Outside the town perimeter and away from the wells the wilderness takes over, mountains loom and Dall sheep roam supreme. Clear crisp water pours through the washouts to feed the turbid Mackenzie River and every year eager fossil hunters arrive in small packs to scour the river beds and open slopes.

Dall sheep roam the rocky terrain of the Mackenzie Mountains.

Upper: *The symmetrical cross section of a fossilized shell is typical of bivalves.*
Lower: *Routed across aluvial planes, up river beds and ridges, the trail to Hammer Mountain results in views of the Mackenzie River and Norman Wells.*

The Dempster Highway winds its way up and down through the Richardson Mountains. This region is characterized by two ecoregions: smooth alpine slopes of tundra at higher elevations, consisting of lichens, mountain avens, dwarf shrubs, sedges and arctic cotton; and valleys of subalpine open woodland vegetation such as stunted spruce, willow, dwarf birch, and Labrador tea with sedge, moss, and arctic cotton in moist depressions.

The Dempster Highway winds its way up and down numerous passes in the Richardson and Ogilvie Mountains, through mostly untouched wilderness between Inuvik at the northern limit of the treeline and Dawson City, deep within the boreal forest. Wide valleys, mountain bands, narrow passes and waterways line the route as it passes through six separate eco-regions of mountains, plateaus and plains.

Grizzlies and black bears can be seen dining on plentiful berries that hug the ground. Porcupine caribou migrate down from the North Slope and across the highway. Such a pristine, ecologically diverse and scenic highway is a treat to enjoy.

The highway was built as a result of an initiative by the Diefenbaker government, known as "Roads to Resources". The name itself is cause to fear for the integrity of this pristine wilderness.

South of Eagle Plains, the vegetation cover of the rounded hills creates a stark contrast to the bare rock features of a band of mountains across the wide valley.

Upper: *Autumn begins as dwarf birch leaves turn red amongst the willows.* Lower: *Views of the Dempster Highway below, cutting straight through alpine tundra, are well worth the hike.*

The Forgotten North hosts a diversity of aboriginal cultures, including Gwich'in, Inuvialuit and Metis, as well as various Dene peoples, such as the Chipewyan, Slavey, Dogrib, Hare, and Nahanni. The richness of their traditional ways persists today, with the people continuing to identify themselves in relationship to the land and the life it supports. Plants and animals provide the food, clothing, tools, and shelter essential to a good life.

Going out on the land is vital to a sense of well-being for these aboriginal cultures, who over centuries have developed a deep connection to, and respect for, the land on which they depend. This includes accepting the responsibility of caring for the land and its living creatures.

Upper: *The day after the first snow, an early morning mist rolls over the mountains north of Eagle Plains on the Dempster Highway.*
Lower: *Alpine vegetation in autumn on the south side of Wright Pass.*

Inuvialuit elder Persis Grueben prepares dry fish. Many traditions of the aboriginal people of the Forgotten North are still practiced today. For people like Persis, the traditional northern lifestyle is part of recent history. As a little girl, she remembers a nomadic subsistence lifestyle and travelling to the supply post and whaling station of Herschel Island.

A steady clicking rhythm begins to fill the air surrounding the congregation, growing louder as more drummers follow the lead and tap their long, slender sticks on the rims of their broad caribou hide drums. Click, click, click, click. Dancers shuffle into the open area as the drummers pick up the volume, beating the entire width of the drum and adding a deep, resonating beat to the clicking. Dancers sweep their arms high and low, their wolverine fur fringes floating through the air. The dancers' souls are possessed by the spirit of their culture and this spirit spreads to the spectators. More and more dancers join in, creating a dizzying pattern of contrasting colour as they sway, dip and spin to the beat of many drums.

It is a time of celebration: a time to gather together, to recount legends and stories of creation, to teach the behaviour of animals and to honour the activities of daily life, such as chopping wood, drawing water, skinning beaver and hunting caribou.

Upper: *A dancer's glove rests on an Inuvialuit drum after the festivity.*
Lower: *Dressed in a traditional parka adorned with Delta Braid and strips of wolverine fur, an elder woman enjoys the spirit of the drum dance.*

The spirit of the Inuvialuit people thrives in the drum dance of the Mackenzie Delta Drummers and Dancers.

From the air or an elevated viewpoint it is relatively easy to trace a route through the maze of lakes and waterways that make up the Mackenzie delta. At water level, it is another world. The terrain is unrelentingly flat, the soil homogeneous and the vegetation uniform. Lofty boreal forest hides the Richardson Mountains from view, eliminating the only terrestrial reference point. Depth perception becomes confused, bearings are lost and even the direction of water flow can be uncertain. Years of experience are the only reliable guide to travel in the world's second largest arctic delta.

Unlike many of the world's great deltas, the 260,000 square kilometre Mackenzie delta is inaccessible and remote, creating a rich ecosystem in which wildlife flourishes. Migratory birds, fur-bearing animals and fish species are found in abundance.

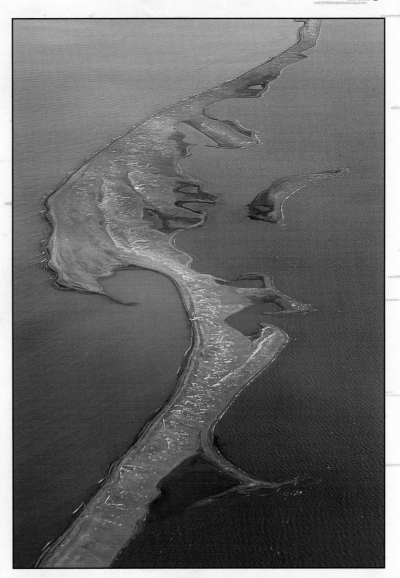

The second largest arctic river delta in the world, the Mackenzie delta's maze of lakes, channels, and main waterways is so complex, it can disorient even the most experienced wilderness travellers.

Sand bars dotted with logs and driftwood mark the transition from the Mackenzie delta to the Beaufort Sea.

Moonrise over the Mackenzie Mountains creates a silver path down the Nahanni River, marking the end of a day's journey in the Forgotten North.

The end of a wilderness journey always seems to be marked by moments of extraordinary natural beauty: an electric pink sunset reflecting off the silver surface of a braided stream on a sand bar in the Thelon River; an encounter with a highly intelligent but very illusive wolverine traveling along the rocky river bank toward our canoe, its little black face peering out from behind a coat of long, flowing blonde hair; the beautiful overlap of moonrise and sunset, casting blues, purples and oranges across the sky, the colours and the breaking clouds reflecting off Four Mile Lake as our float plane descends to land; or the gathering of fifty loons around our boat, the sound of their calls echoing back and forth through the mist rising from the surface of the lake.

Often it is the last spectacular landscape of a journey that is etched in my mind, like the aerial view of the intricate butterscotch artistry of the William River as it meanders past the Athabasca Sand Dunes, or an autumn vista along the Dempster Highway, the multitude of bright colours against a smooth, sloping mountain backdrop.

Nostalgia sweeps over me as I retrace my steps and recount experiences at each leg of the journey - the stunning landscapes, the minute details of special rocks and plants, encounters with animals that seemed to communicate with me, the intimate friendships that developed between fellow travelers, and the feeling of reconnecting with the earth.

Although I find comfort in aspects of urban society, I always relive journeys of the past in my mind, in my photographs and in sharing experiences with others. Meanwhile, the wilderness beckons, urging me to make plans for the next journey.

In the darkness of the winter's afternoon, ptarmigan take flight like vanishing ghosts, evoking a sense of spirit within. They are like messengers of nature, sent to impress the spirit of the wilderness on the souls of all human beings, reconnecting us to the earth and to our part of the whole.

Leslie Leong

A four-day snowmobile trip has barely begun when Leslie abruptly stops her machine, grabs her camera and aims at a snowy white ptarmigan hiding motionless beside the trail. The ptarmigan is camera-shy and moves deeper into the adjacent shrubland. As I watch in amusement, Leslie struggles after the cautious bird, wading through waist-deep snow in her bulky parka and soft leather mukluks, hoping for just the right angle and light conditions. The ptarmigan stays just out of range, its feathery feet walking easily on the soft snow. Forty-five minutes later the ptarmigan finally relents, having decided that this slow-moving, two-legged beast is really quite harmless. Leslie wades back to the trail, a triumphant smile on her face.

Outstanding photography takes not only a keen eye and a sense of artistic balance, but also determination, persistence and passion. Every photo in Leslie's collection is not only a work of art but the result of countless hours of planning and packing, and weeks of remote isolation and natural hazards. Each photo is more than an isolated scene. It is a snapshot of the ongoing and enjoyable process that is the life of this talented photographer.

In the 25 years I have known Leslie, she has applied this same dedication to her travels. She took her first pictures on a trip along the newly opened Dempster Highway in 1979, where a sign still warned travelers that there was "No fuel, food or lodging for 542km." Subsequent trips took her throughout Taiwan, Turkey and Europe. Leslie's sense of adventure also lead her far into Canada's back country, including Baffin Island. Intrigued by the north, Leslie found a job in the Northwest Territories that combined her civil engineering background with her love for wilderness.

Leslie became a full-time photographer in 1994 and now devotes her time to recording natural beauty and diversity, hoping to instill in others her passion and spiritual attachment to the environment.

Detmar Schwichtenberg

Photo: Nigel Allan

CANADA'S
Northwest Territories
A Land of Diversity

Photographer and Writer
Leslie Leong

Text Editor
Detmar Schwichtenberg

Research, Design and Publishing
Leslie Leong Ent. Ltd.

Printer
Kromar Printing Ltd.

Photo: Lillian Leong

Photo: Terry Best

Upper: *Leslie Leong has been living in the Northwest Territories since 1991.*
Lower Left: *Leslie observes gyrfalcon fledglings at Hawk Rock on the Hanbury River.*
Lower Right: *Leslie photographing shield country in winter.*